FAIRACRES PUBLICATIONS 215

PRAYER
Too Deep
for Words

Sister Edmée slg

SLG Press

Fairacres Publications 215

ISBN 978-0-7283-0388-1
Fairacres Publications Series ISSN 0307-1405

Edited and typeset in Palatino Linotype by Julia Craig-McFeely

Biblical quotations are taken from the New Revised Standard Version of
the Bible unless otherwise noted.

ACKNOWLEDGEMENT
The translation from John the Solitary is reprinted by kind permission
of the Editors, *The Journal of Theological Studies*, Oxford University Press.

SLG Press
Convent of the Incarnation
Fairacres • Oxford
www.slgpress.co.uk

Printed by
Grosvenor Group Ltd, Loughton, Essex

CONTENTS

PREFACE

Sister Edmée had been a dancer and modelled for Vogue before the circumstances of her life and her friendships led her to the church. Her early experiences gave her a unique outlook and also a particular sense of humour; she was a strong character, feisty, passionate about what she saw to be right, with a sharp and often critical mind, and a pointed turn of phrase. She said that at the point when she joined the Anglican church meaning entered her life, and her pilgrimage had begun, leading her in 1966 to join the community of the Sisters of the Love of God. Fr David Barton came to know her well as Warden of the order while she was writing her doctoral study on the Song of Songs; in his address at her funeral in 2018, he said:

> what she had learned from her community was to 'keep on going on … As we learn to shoulder the task that is in front of us and are faithful to it, so we begin to sense the grace of God working in us.' That awareness of the centrality of grace is characteristic. Her dedication of 'the Way of the Cross' was a deliberate choice. She always battled with herself.

Although her life in the convent was removed from most people's ordinary existence, the level of her interest both in world affairs and in other individuals meant that she was very involved in many lives, bearing people in mind and paying them attention, even if she had never met and would never meet them. In publishing four books of her shorter writings in 2024, SLG Press brings the fruits of her prayer and study, and her particular voice to those who did not know her in life.

PRAYER
Too Deep
for Words

Prayer, the Work of the Spirit

> Likewise the Spirit helps us in our weakness; for we do not
> know how to pray as we ought, but that very Spirit intercedes
> with sighs too deep for words. And God, who searches the
> heart, knows what is the mind of the Spirit, because the Spirit
> intercedes for the saints according to the will of God.
>
> (Rom. 8:26–7)

This passage from St Paul's Letter to the Romans is very familiar
and I am sure we feel we know what it means. We would agree,
for instance, that we do not know how to pray as we ought, and
we would readily concede that we would do much better if the
Spirit would indeed come to help us in our weakness. But the
Spirit, speaking in Jesus, said: 'apart from me you can do nothing.' (John 15:5) Not, as we naturally incline to think, 'apart
from me you can do a surprising amount if only you would try
harder' but 'apart from me you can do *nothing*'. Therefore, without the Spirit we cannot pray at all; and the Spirit prays within
us, according to St Paul, in a way that is 'too deep for words'
(Rom. 8:26).

If this is so, then prayer is not quite what we imagine it
ideally to be. We have a picture of perfect prayer, that is to say,
of a person in prayer, whose heart is suffused with loving devo-
tion and whose mind, deeply recollected, is presenting to God in
orderly fashion the traditional components of prayer: adoration,
confession, intercession, petition, and thanksgiving. Moreover,
with such a picture, prayer is regarded as something we do and
therefore becomes another thing to be done, yet another demand
on our time, another activity to be fitted into a full day. But, in

truth, prayer is something that is done within us, the very opposite of another activity, for it is the activity of Another.

But is that not precisely why we find it so difficult to stop for it? If it were another of our activities would we not, in our generosity, make time for it, since this activity is for God? Prayer, the kind of which St Paul speaks, which is too deep for words, and is not ours anyway, is of its nature in direct opposition to the whole movement of our life—and this is where the difficulty in stopping for it lies. I have heard it said that if a person falls overboard from a large ocean-going liner it takes four hours for the ship to return to the spot: two hours to stop and two hours to retrace the distance it has covered since it began to stop. That is very often how stopping for prayer feels! We are going full steam ahead with, no doubt, a full cargo of good works, and nothing less than a catastrophe can make us turn round, turn to God. However, though our turning is the work of a moment, the forces against us can, under ordinary circumstances, seem quite as great as those which make stopping an ocean liner so laboured.

But if we want to pray we have to stop. It is very simple—and very difficult. Very simple because in order to pray that is *all* we have to do; very difficult because stopping requires a special kind of effort for which we will receive help neither from our nature nor from our circumstances. And if our circumstances include small children we may feel that efforts to stop—special or otherwise—are out of the question.

But are they? If God desires to draw us into a closer relationship with himself, will he be content to wait until the children have started school, or even until they have left home? No, he wants us *now*, in the midst of our impossible circumstances. In that case, you may say, let him make those circumstances a little less impossible. That is, indeed, the tone to which he responds. 'Now look here, God... ' is an approach which, at least in my experience, always gains his attention, and I think the secret of it is that in using it we are looking to him for the answer instead of looking to ourselves. There seems to be an instinct that leads us to think that before we can expect God to order our lives we must put them in order ourselves first. No, for 'It is *all* his work', as Fr Gilbert Shaw used to say. But the truth of this simple statement is not so simply understood. Moreover, our efforts to make time for God do indeed seem to have an unaided quality about them so that his work in the matter is not at all obvious. This may be because time itself has been given to us by God as the framework in which our free will can operate. Reginald Somerset Ward, another great director of souls, taught that 'A rule of life is primarily concerned with time, the only possession we have in this world.'[1] Somehow then, we have to learn to manage time—a subject on which Archbishop Anthony Bloom writes vividly:

> ... learn to manage time, not when it is moving in a sluggish, meandering way, but at the moment when it is trying to rush like water from a burst pipe. It is simply a matter of saying at the moment when you are busy with something useful which must be done: 'I stop doing this, I'll keep still an instant and remain alone with God!' ... Settle peacefully and say: 'Whatever happens, I will not budge.' Say to all those, visible and invisible, who come to disturb you: 'I am very sorry; I am here, but not for you!'[2]

That is all very well, I can hear someone say, but my children start murdering each other, or setting the place on fire, or negotiating themselves into a position from which they can hurl themselves into the afterlife the moment I try to settle peacefully! Yes, it is easy for those of us who have withdrawn ourselves from

---

[1] [Reginald Somerset Ward], *Following The Way: Devotional Studies in Mystical Religion* (St Christopher Press, 1928), 165.
[2] Anthony Bloom, 'Holiness and Prayer' in *God and Man* (DLT, 1971), 105.

the overwhelming commitments of rearing children, and the problems of secular life in general, to talk about finding spaces for prayer. Nevertheless, perhaps because we are not in the forest we may be able to point to the clearings. The clearings are found, I believe, when we begin to understand what is in our nature, quite apart from our circumstances, which is contrary to prayer; that is, contrary to silence, stillness and surrender. Circumstances merely reinforce and justify nature, so when our circumstances are dominated by children (for example) the problems of our nature are more readily masked because they become externalized in those beings whose nature it is to reflect our own.

Parents, then, are fighting a double battle if they desire to pray: a battle with their own natures, and a battle with that same nature as reflected back to them by their offspring. In other words, the battle is not, as it appears to be on the surface, with the nature of the child. To understand this requires a great deal of self-observation; moreover it may not be entirely true. It does appear that the natural tendency of children to be by turns 'little demons' and 'little angels' is not unconnected with the state of the parent; a little demon often being the consequence of that ceaseless action/reaction with a parent who is not fully present to the child in peaceful attention, and a little angel being the response when they are. If this is so, at least in the most general terms, it can be seen that times for prayer and silence are not to be wrenched out of the day in spite of the children, but rather *for the sake of the children*. A parent who can withdraw themselves at times from the constant and insistent needs of their children is meeting those needs at another level; the firm purpose required will give them a sense of security in their parents (or parent) and in life as experienced through them which they are unlikely ever to lose.

Having then struggled with circumstances and against nature, and, let us suppose, being peacefully settled and determined not to budge for any of those, visible and invisible, who will come to disturb you, what then? Let us return to Archbishop Anthony:

> If you sit down in a room and say to yourself: 'I am in the presence of God', you will see that at the end of a moment you will be wondering how to fill this presence with an activity that will suppress your restlessness. For the first few moments you will feel fine because you are tired and it is a rest to be sitting comfortably in an armchair, and the silence of your room gives you a feeling of quietude. All this is true. But if you have to go beyond this moment of natural rest, and you remain in the presence of God when you have already received from physical nature all that you can get from it, you will see that it is very difficult not to wonder: 'And now what shall I do? What should I say to God? How shall I address Him? He is silent. Is He there? How can I make a bridge between that mute absence and my restless presence?'[3]

So one of the first things to understand is the importance of sitting and doing nothing in front of God.

The importance of sitting and doing nothing in front of God is to allow him to do something in us. So we surrender ourselves to him in the moment of sitting down; physically this means that we allow our natural energies to run down and our thoughts to drop away so that we become still, both feet on the floor, shoulders down, hands and face relaxed (or however we choose to place ourselves for this peaceful moment). 'I appeal to you, therefore, brothers and sisters,' writes St Paul,

> by the mercies of God, to present your bodies as a living sacrifice, holy and acceptable to God, which is your spiritual worship. Do not be conformed to this world, but be transformed by the renewing of your minds, that you may discern what is the will of God – what is good and acceptable and perfect.
>
> (Rom. 12:1–2)

---

[3] Bloom, *God and Man*, 105.

This transformation by the renewal of our mind is entirely the work of the Spirit, and our efforts should be gently directed towards opening a space for the Spirit in the mind rather than trying to force efforts from it. Jean-Nicolas Grou, a seventeenth-century French writer on spirituality whose teaching on prayer is among the finest, expounds this matter with vigour:

> We easily lose sight of the truth that [prayer] is a supernatural act, which consequently is above our strength ... Thus St Paul says: 'Not that we are sufficient of ourselves to claim anything as coming from us, but our sufficiency is from God.' (2 Cor. 3:5) ... Now if we are to expect all from God, all our good thoughts and all our good feelings, how is it that ... some people are so indiscreet as to strain their heads, get agitated, and work up their imagination as if all depended on their own efforts? As prayer is a supernatural act we must earnestly entreat of God that He would bring it about in our heart and then we must peacefully make it under His direction ... But [the Abbé Grou continues, replying for the reader], my heart says nothing to me when I am in the presence of God; if I wish to enter into myself I find nothing but a void, dryness, distractions. To fill up my time, to excite feelings of devotion, to withdraw my mind from troublesome thoughts, I must absolutely make use of a book. But do you not see that the high-flown sentiments that you borrow from books act only on your imagination; that they are not your own, or rather only seem to be your own for the moment? You are reading them, and once the book is closed you are just as dry, just as cold as before. Nevertheless I have prayed, say you, while reading or reciting these formulae. Your self-love thinks so and is satisfied; but is God's judgment the same as yours? Is God equally satisfied? What does He care for words, He who listens only to the heart?[4]

---

[4] Abbé Jean-Nicolas Grou SJ, *How to Pray*, trans. by Teresa Fitzgerald, ed. and with a preface by Father [Richard Frederick] Clarke (London: Thomas Baker, 2nd edn, 1901), 5–6.

Grou's manner of berating the reader may partly explain why he is not as much read nowadays as he deserves to be. Moreover such a supreme authority on prayer as St Teresa of Ávila, writing in her *Life*, seems to say the opposite on the subject of reading in prayer time:

> During [eighteen] years, except after communicating, I never dared to begin to pray without a book; my soul was as much afraid to engage in prayer without one as if it were having to go and fight against a host of enemies. With this help, which was a companionship to me and a shield with which I could parry the blows of my many thoughts, I felt comforted. For it was not usual with me to suffer from aridity; this only came when I had no book, whereupon my soul would at once become disturbed and my thoughts would begin to wander. As soon as I started to read they began to collect themselves and the book acted like a bait to my soul.[5]

This passage, however, is written in the context of Teresa's explanations regarding her inability to arouse her imagination according to prescribed methods of meditation, and she concludes with relief that it was the Lord's good providence which spared her during those eighteen years from being subject to a director who, as she says, might have insisted on cutting her off from the succours which reading gives. Reading, indeed, is crucial to the spiritual life, for the Spirit speaks to us through what we read, and we need a great deal of such speaking *to* us if we are ever to learn how to let him speak *in* us. Nevertheless, Père Grou is making a number of immensely important points, so let us press on with him:

> If it is the heart that prays, evidently it can sometimes and even habitually pray alone, without words, either expressed or men-

---

[5] Teresa of Ávila, *Life*, book IV, in *The Complete Works of St Teresa of Ávila*, trans. and ed. by Edgar Allison Peers, vol. 3 (Sheed & Ward Ltd, 1957), 24.

tal. This is just what few people understand and many deny altogether. They must have express and formal acts, at least interior, that are distinctly perceived, and of which the soul is conscious; without such acts they recognise no prayer. They are however mistaken and God has not yet taught them how the heart prays. It prays in the same way as the mind thinks. Now thought is formed in the mind before it can be clothed in words. The proof of this is that words are often sought and one after another rejected till the words are met with that best express our thought. We want words to make ourselves understood by others; but they are useless for ourselves, and if we were pure spirits we should need no language either for the formation or for the communication of our thoughts. So it is with the feelings of the heart; it conceives them, it adopts them, and puts them in practice, without there being any necessity of words, unless it would communicate them to our fellow men, or bear testimony of them to ourselves.

God reads the secrets of our heart; He penetrates into the very depths of our most intimate feelings, even of those not reflected upon, or perceived even by the soul ... But people treat with God as they do with men, thinking they are not understood unless they go into detailed explanations of the things they require. They carefully get ready their intention; they have express forms for each and every act, they name separately each person they wish to pray for, and if the least detail escapes their memory they do not think that God can supply it. Souls of little faith, and who know not God, your intentions are present to Him before you open your mouth! He sees them as soon as they are formed in your heart; what need have you to torment yourselves in explaining them to Him? You desire all spiritual blessings as much for yourselves as for those in whom you take an interest. Is He ignorant of this, since He Himself inspires you with these desires? Do not then have any anxiety, concerning this matter. If you feel drawn to this simple and general prayer of which I speak, do not give it up under the pretext that it aims at no particular object, that you come from it without having asked for anything. Here again you are deceiving yourself; you have asked for everything you need for yourself and for those belonging to you far better than if you had specified each want of which the multiplicity would only have wearied you and hindered the action of God ...[6]

In these passages from Grou we have the character of contemplative prayer clearly set forth: a supernatural activity which consequently is beyond our capacity to perform, and which takes place in the innermost chamber of the soul where words are not needed for communication, and where what is happening between the soul and God is not perceived even, as Grou tells us, by the soul itself.

Although words are not needed by the soul they are needed by the mind, for the mind is not engaged in such prayer and is therefore free to follow its natural bent, that is, to chatter ceaselessly—and it will, we cannot stop it. What we can do is to provide it with simple phrases from Scripture, especially from the Psalms. 'O God, you are my God, I seek you' (Ps. 63:1) is an example, and there are hundreds of others from the same treasury. The Jesus Prayer, 'Lord Jesus Christ, have mercy on me a sinner' is a phrase from the Orthodox East which is now used very widely in the West.[7] Many Christians, following the recommendation of the author of *The Cloud of Unknowing*, are content simply to repeat the word 'God'.[8] Whatever word or form of words we use, the mind

---

[6] Abbé Grou, *How to Pray*, 8–13.

[7] The most widely used introduction to the Jesus Prayer now is Kallistos Ware, *The Power of the Name*, Fairacres Publications 43 (SLG Press, 1974, rev. 1986, 13/2013). Other helpful short texts published recently include: Bruce Batstone, *Still Listening: Sowing the Seeds of the Jesus Prayer*, Fairacres Publications 206 (SLG Press 2023); James F. Wellington, *Journeying with the Jesus Prayer*, Fairacres Publications 186 (SLG Press 2020); Simon Barrington-Ward, *The Jesus Prayer* (The Bible Reading Fellowship, 2007).

[8] *The Cloud of Unknowing and Other Works*, ed. and trans. by A. Spearing (Penguin Classics, 2001).

will run hither and thither and deprive us of any concrete sense that we are engaged in prayer. Nevertheless, it is our *intention* with which God engages, not our *attention*. John Cassian, one of the earliest commentators on Christian monasticism in the fourth century, writes: 'It is not a perfect prayer in which the monk is conscious of himself or understands his prayer',[9] and a similar saying, attributed to St Antony of Padua, the Father of monks, puts it even more strongly: 'He prays best who does not know he is praying.' As regards advice, the best of all is an anonymous saying from the end of the twentieth century: 'If you spend half an hour gently returning the mind to God you will have spent the time very well.'[10]

[9] *John Cassian: The Conferences*, trans. and annotated by Boniface Ramsey (Newman Press, 1997), from no. XXXI, on p. 349, referring to St Anthony of the Desert.

[10] First attributed to St Francis de Sales in 1996, but cannot be traced in any of his writings.

MARY AND THE MYSTERY OF PRAYER

What about the rest of life? Clearly times set apart for prayer are not in themselves enough for the growth of prayer. A chapter in the SLG states that 'the prayer which the Sisters carry out in chapel or cell is not regarded as a contrast to, but as a continuing expression of, the corporate offering', and it continues: 'Ideally the whole life is to be made prayer.'[11] What does this mean? Thomas Merton has provided a key text on this subject:

> It is above all in this silent witness and unconscious testimony to the love of God that the contemplative exercises his apostolate. For the saint preaches sermons by the way he walks and the way he stands and the way he sits down and the way he picks things up and holds them in his hand.[12]

The ideal this passage presents may seem too from the reality of daily life to be worth quoting. Yet every Christian, whatever their circumstances, is called to exercise their apostolate primarily by showing forth the state of their being. No amount of doing can make up for the absence of being. But if we are to have any being to show forth we need times of silence and stillness. There is much in contemporary secular life which is unavoidable, but there is even more that is not; for instance, the misuse of the broadcast media as merely background so that instead of refreshing our energies they are drained, and the use of

---

[11] SLG Rule, Ch. 16: 'Prayer', from the sub-section on 'Non-Liturgical Prayer'. The SLG Rule is available on the website of the Community of the Sisters of the Love of God: https://slg.org.uk/who-we-are/the-rule/
[12] Thomas Merton, *Seeds of Contemplation* (New Directions, 1949), 116.

social media to fill times that would otherwise be for inaction and thought. The result, then, is that we lack the power to be present in our actions; to be present in our walking, our standing, our sitting down, and in our handling not only of things but of people, and of everything which should be the means of our making our whole life an offering of worship to God.

All this brings us to Our Lady, the Blessed Virgin Mary, Mother of God, the type of the contemplative for every age. For Mary is best understood not as the model for any person's role in society but as the symbol of the soul's response to God. '"Be it done unto me according to thy word." And she conceived by the Holy Spirit.'[13]

It is through pondering on the mystery of Mary that we come to understand the mystery of prayer: that it is nothing other than a total surrender to the activity of the Holy Spirit within us. In an article written by A. M. Allchin there is passage with which I should like to conclude as I believe what it says to be immensely important for this subject.

> Mary, the Mother of God, reminds us of the necessity for silence, receptivity, growth and contemplation. At times in our century, the Church seems to be running along behind the world ... desperately trying to present to the world a mirror-image of its own concerns. But unless the Church can reveal to our society something which it does not already know or does not recognise about itself, what value has it for the world, let alone in the eyes of God? In the world itself, if we would be attentive to it, there are many hints of a growing awareness of the need to rediscover the intuitive, symbolical, pre-conscious modes of living and knowing and being, the need to find some corrective to the insistent pressures of activity. Is it not the Church which ought to be able to give to the world the possibility of a new vision, of a new framework in which to see things? Perhaps what we need above all is the ability to

---

[13] Luke 1:38 and Matthew 1:18 paraphrased in the *Angelus*.

wait and to listen, to be present and open, to let things grow, so that our actions may in time become more fruitful and less anxious, and our words be qualified with the wisdom which comes from silence. It may be that the reason why for many, Catholic as well as Protestant, the question of Mary seems remote and unimportant, is because the particular things for which Mary stands are neither seen nor understood. It seems as if we were trying to incarnate the presence of God in the world through our own efforts, without sufficiently realising that if it is to be the presence of *God*, and not just of certain ideas, or words, or concepts about God, then that presence can only become real in our world, in our flesh, in so far as we are learning to be open, receptive, obedient to the Word of God, so that the Holy Spirit may work his recreative work in us. Only in the free consent and obedience of the Virgin could God take flesh; only through his relationship to her, could her Son, who is God's Son, express in human love the love of God which both creates and redeems the world. Only in so far as the Church and every member of it begins to rediscover how she, the second Eve, is the mother of all living shall we be able again not only to confess our faith before the world, but to live it in simplicity and joy.[14]

---

[14] A. M. Allchin, 'Mary, Virgin and Mother: An Anglican Approach', *Marian Library Studies* 1 (1969), 96–112.

Silence in Prayer

Silence shall always be regarded as one of the chief privileges of the Community, for it prepares the way for the union of the soul with the will of God and is an offering of perpetual reverence to his majesty. It is in silence that the spirit will be trained to deepen recollection and to exercise itself after the likeness of the Seraphim and Cherubim that worship round the throne of God. But it should be remembered that silence must cover all the levels of the conscious life; there must be an outward silence of speech and movement, a silence of the mind for the overcoming of vain imaginations and distractions, and a silence of the soul in the surrender of the will to be still and know that God is God, leading to a silence of spirit which is the preparation for the fulness of contemplation.

That passage comes from the chapter on silence in the SLG Rule. It is a key passage, not only in that particular chapter but in the Rule as a whole. Spending time in a monastic community allows people for a few hours to taste the quality of a life which regards silence as one of its chief privileges, and so return refreshed, we hope, to the natural clamour of a world which cannot be organized with silence as its keystone to the same extent. Nevertheless, properly understood, silence belongs as much to everyone's life as it does to the religious, and in the following pages I hope to consider ways in which that claim may be realized, firstly by considering the question of silence in prayer and secondly the question of silence in action, regarding prayer and action as distinct, like the persons of the Trinity, but, so to speak, one in being; that is, united by the silence from which both true prayer and true action proceed.

Before considering silence in prayer we might first question the whole notion of the desirability of silence. What is so good about it? Why do we regard silence as one of the chief privileges of a monastic Community? Is it really the preparation for the union of the soul with the will of God? Are there not thousands, even millions, of Christians living in the light of the Gospel whose lives altogether lack silence and who know nothing of the practice of silence in prayer? Yes, very probably. But whatever may or may not be true of others will be irrelevant on that Great Day when we are required to answer for every idle word! It is not possible to judge our fellow-Christians on this question, but I think we may say that where silence in prayer is not being practised something vital to the Christian life is not being developed.

In every Christian life there should be a two- or three-fold development of the work of the Holy Spirit through baptism, and these developments could be seen in terms of distinct calls: the 'common', the 'particular' and the 'unique'. The 'common' call begins at baptism and grows, through grace, until we are drawn to make a conscious decision to live in accordance with our baptismal vows. This 'common' call is all-embracing; it cannot be superseded in any sense; there is nothing 'higher'. The SLG Rule recognizes this in its opening paragraph: 'All Christians are called through baptism to sanctification in a life of total commitment to the service of God'.[15] However within this 'common' call, sanctification in a life of total commitment will require, for some Christians, a response to the 'particular' — the call to the priesthood or the religious life, for instance. But for all Christians there is the 'unique' call, that is, the call to develop a unique relationship with the God who made each one of us in his image and likeness, and on whom, in this 'unique' stage, we become wholly dependent and thus uniquely and wonderfully ourselves, filling a place in relation both to God and

---

[15] Ch. 1 'The Monastic State'.

to our fellow creatures which only we and none other can fill. This secret and ultimate vocation to realize our uniqueness can only, I believe, be developed in silence before God. It is here we are given a foretaste of that final fulfilment expressed by the Psalmist that 'when I awake I shall be satisfied, beholding your likeness' (Ps. 17:15).

This, then, is what is so good about silence, for it is in silence that we come to ourselves and arise for the return journey to our heavenly home. We see, moreover, that the 'common' and the 'unique' calls are the essential ones. This is important to understand, for what can happen, wherever religion is structured to provide places for the 'particular', is that the 'common' Christian who has not been called to the particular can be held back from entering the 'unique' by the assumption that the particular call, far from being merely intermediary, is the ultimate and therefore superior one. When those called to the particular themselves believe this they are liable to fall under our Lord's condemnation:

> But woe to you, scribes and Pharisees, hypocrites! For you lock people out of the kingdom of heaven. For you do not go in yourselves, and when others are going in, you stop them. (Matt. 23:13)

Wherever the blame lies, the 'common' Christian who is not entering the 'unique', will either settle down into the structure—sadly or smugly, according to temperament (and any PCC provides rich material for the study of the 'common' Christian—the self-deprecating sidesman, for instance, who claims to be just a simple bloke, not like the Vicar—and so on); or they will react against the particular call and either ignore the structure that provides for it (and go off to study a different religion, perhaps) or become belligerent about it, and even try in some way or other to muscle in on it.

Likewise, the person who has responded to the particular call can come to feel equally shut out of the kingdom if they do not understand that there is more to their life than being, for instance, a priest. They can become stuck in their role, and if that happens they will be prone to frustrations and excessive sensitivity to the seeming fatuities of ecclesiastical superiors—who may also be stuck in the particular—or be over-confident in the interpretation of the priestly ministry and, by assuming authority for themselves, fail to mediate the authority of the One they are serving.

These are dangers which attend the particular call if we think, in responding to it, that we have 'done all'. No, we are still unprofitable servants; we have only done that which it was our duty to do.[16] There remains our unique call to answer. But we answer it not in order to be taken beyond the particular—rather the contrary. We answer it to be better able to fulfil the particular. I know that if I were to abandon my particular call, the pursuit of the unique would be sheer illusion. So it is right for us to be identified with our particular call. A deeply moving example of this right identification was the simple response, 'I am a priest', to the question, 'Who are you?' when Maximilian Kolbe stepped forward to offer himself for the death cell in place of another prisoner.[17] He might have said, 'I am Maximilian Kolbe', or 'I am a Franciscan friar', or even, to his German interrogator, 'I am a Pole'. But in that moment, everything both common and unique in him was wholly concentrated in the particular—his priesthood. Thus the sacrifice of his life became the consummation of his priestly ministry; and by his sacrifice he ministered throughout that terrible fortnight not only to his fellow-condemned but to the whole camp. And he continues, in the communion of saints, to mediate his priesthood by his confession of it in the face of death.

---

[16] Cf. Luke 17:10.

[17] André Frossard, *Forget Not Love: The Passion of Maximilian Kolbe* (Ignatius Press, 1991), 197.

So now we turn to consider the unique—that which I have
suggested can only be developed in silence. Let us start by div-
ing into the deep end with a long extract from a letter on prayer
by John the Solitary, a Syrian monk who lived, it is thought, in
the fifth century:

> Do not imagine, brother, that prayer consists solely of words,
> or that it can be learnt by means of words. No, the truth of the
> matter, you should understand, is that spiritual prayer does not
> reach fulness as a result of either learning or the repetition of
> words. For it is not to a man that you are praying, before whom
> you can repeat a well-composed speech; it is to Him who is
> Spirit that you are directing the movements of your prayer. You
> should pray therefore in spirit, seeing that He is Spirit.
>
> No special place is required for someone who prays in ful-
> ness to God. Our Lord said, 'The hour is coming when you will
> not be worshipping the Father in this mountain or in Jerusalem';
> and again, to show that no special place was required, he also
> taught that those who worship the Father should 'worship Him
> in spirit and in truth'; and in the course of his instructing us why
> we should pray thus he said, 'For God is a Spirit', and He should
> be praised spiritually, in the spirit. Paul too tells us about this
> spiritual prayer and psalmody which we should employ: 'What
> then shall I do?', he says, 'I will pray in spirit and pray in my
> mind; I will sing in the spirit and I will sing in my mind'. It is in
> spirit and in mind, then, that he says one should pray and sing
> to God; he does not say anything at all about the tongue. The
> reason is that this spiritual prayer is more interior than the
> tongue, more deeply interiorized than anything on the lips,
> more interiorized than any words or vocal song. When someone
> prays this kind of prayer he has sunk deeper than all speech,
> and he stands where spiritual beings and angels are to be found;
> like them he utters 'holy' without any words …
>
> For God is silence, and in silence is He sung by means of
> that psalmody which is worthy of Him. I am not speaking of the
> silence of the tongue, for if someone merely keeps his tongue si-
> lent, without knowing how to sing in mind and spirit, then he

is simply unoccupied and becomes filled with evil thoughts; he
is just keeping an exterior silence and he does not know how to
sing in an interior way, seeing that the tongue of his 'hidden
man' has not yet learnt to stretch itself out even to babble. You
should look on the spiritual infant that is within you in the same
way as you do on an ordinary child or infant; just as the tongue
placed in an infant's mouth is still because it does not yet know
speech or the right movements for speaking, so it is with that
interior tongue of the mind; it will be still from all speech and
from all thought; it will simply be placed there, ready to learn
the first babblings of spiritual utterance.

Thus there is a silence of the tongue, there is a silence of the
whole body, there is the silence of the soul, there is the silence of
the mind, and there is the silence of the spirit. The silence of the
tongue is merely when it is not incited to evil speech; the silence
of the entire body is when all its senses are unoccupied; the silence of the soul is when there are not ugly thoughts bursting
forth within it; the silence of the mind is when it is not reflecting
on any harmful knowledge or wisdom; the silence of the spirit is
when the mind ceases even from stirrings caused by created spiritual beings and all its movements are stirred solely by Being, at
the wondrous awe of the silence which surrounds Being.

These are the degrees and measures to be found in speech
and silence. But if you have not reached these and find yourself
still far away from them, remain where you are and sing to
God using the voice and the tongue in love and awe. Stand in
awe of God, as is only right, and you will thus be held worthy
to love Him with a pure love—Him who was given to us at our
renewal [baptism] ...[18]

That is all very simple—yet it is very difficult too. In order
to expand some of its points I shall use another substantial extract from the Eastern tradition, this time nearer home and by
a near contemporary, Kallistos Ware, from a paper he wrote

---

[18] Sebastian Brock, trans., 'John the Solitary, On Prayer', *Journal of
Theological Studies* (April 1979), 97–9.

called 'Silence in Prayer: The Meaning of Hesychia'.[19] The full sense of this word *hesychia* unfolds during the course of the paper, but in principle, Ware explains, it is a general term for inward prayer, and a hesychast is one who practises such prayer, while hesychasm, of course, refers to the prayer itself. The following extract begins at the section entitled 'Hesychia and Spiritual Poverty':

> Inward stillness, when interpreted as a guarding of the heart and a return into oneself, implies a passage from multiplicity to unity, from diversity to simplicity and spiritual poverty. To use the terminology of Evagrius, the mind must become 'naked'. This aspect of *hesychia* is made explicit in another definition provided by St John Climacus: '*Hesychia* is a laying aside of thoughts'. Here he is adapting an Evagrian phrase, 'Prayer is a laying aside of thoughts'. *Hesychia* involves a progressive self-emptying, in which the mind is stripped of all visual images and man-made concepts, and so contemplates in purity the realm of God …
>
> This 'pure silence', although it is termed 'spiritual poverty', is far from being a mere absence or privation. If the hesychast strips his mind of all man-made concepts, so far as this is possible, his aim in this 'self-noughting' is altogether constructive—that he may be filled with an all-embracing sense of the Divine indwelling. The point is well made by St Gregory of Sinai: 'Why speak at length? Prayer is God, who works all things in men'. Prayer is God; it is not primarily something which I do but something which God is doing in me—'not I, but Christ in me'. The hesychast programme is exactly delineated in the words of the Baptist concerning the Messiah: 'He must increase, but I must decrease'. The hesychast ceases from his own activity, not in order to be idle, but in order to enter into the activity of God. His silence is not vacant and negative— a blank pause between words, a short rest before resuming

[19] 'Silence in Prayer: The Meaning of Hesychia', in Bernadette Dieker and Jonathan Montaldo, eds., *Merton and Hesychasm* (Fons Vitae, 2003).

speech—but intensely positive: an attitude of alert attentiveness, of vigilance, and above all of *listening*. The hesychast is *par excellence* the one who *listens*, who is open to the presence of Another: 'Be still and know that I am God' … Returning into himself, the hesychast enters the secret chamber of his own heart in order that, standing there before God, he may listen to the wordless speech of his Creator. 'When you pray', observes a contemporary Orthodox writer in Finland, 'you yourself must be silent; let the prayer speak'—more exactly, let God speak … Understood in these terms, as an entering into the life and the activity of God, *hesychia* is something which during this present age men can achieve only to a limited and imperfect degree. It is an eschatological reality, reserved in its fulness for the Age to Come. In the words of St Isaac: 'Silence is a symbol of the future world'.[20]

In those two extracts from John the Solitary and Kallistos Ware we are told *what* to do and *why* we should do it—that we should lay aside all thoughts so that we may listen in silence to God's wordless voice speaking within us, becoming passive to him that he might be active in us. But there is more to be said on *how* we should do it and on what actually happens when we attempt to attain silence in prayer.

First of all, one of the paradoxes of pure prayer is that we suppose we shall become aware only of God but find, in the laying aside of thoughts, that we become aware instead of our own body. This is wholly right. It is now that we discover the perfect unity which exists between body, mind and spirit, and that the least lack of surrender in any of these parts is at once reflected in all of them. It is indeed something of a chicken-and-egg question as to which comes first: tensions in the body producing

---

[20] Published in Basil Pennington, ed., *One Yet Two: Monastic tradition, East and West*, Proceedings of the Orthodox-Cistercian Symposium, Oxford University 26 August–1 September 1973 (Cistercian Publications, 1976), 30–3.

tensions in the mind and spirit, or tensions in the mind or spirit producing tensions in the body. Until the last few years the problem of how to dispose the body in prayer so that it may be as free from tensions as possible has not been much discussed in the Western Christian tradition. But with the penetration of Eastern ideas some welcome light has been shed on it, and in *Prayer and Contemplation*, Robert Llewelyn, a priest who has spent several years in India, gives some helpful instructions, as the following extract will, I think, show:

> The basic requirement in posture is that the back should be held straight in an easy tension. This applies in whatever position we adopt—whether we stand, sit or kneel upright; or kneel sitting on the heels, perhaps with the help of a cushion or prayer stool … The rule should be to adopt whatever position we can maintain without undue strain. Let us assume we have chosen to sit on an upright chair. Holding the back straight in an easy tension will assist a natural counter-relaxation of the temples and forehead, and the muscles of the face and jaw. The mouth should be shut, but not tightly so; the eyes closed and relaxed … the hands resting palms downwards on the upper part of the thighs, or palms upwards in the lap. The classic position for the head is erect, firmly set on the neck, the back, neck and head forming one straight line … I believe there is value in knowing and saying these things but I would not wish to be over-assertive about them. I have great respect for the approach of *The Cloud of Unknowing*, which is to lay down no rules but simply allow the body to straighten out naturally to its correct position as the prayer proceeds. Yet I am sure there is need for this other approach as well, and it must be left to the individual to find the right balance between the two.[21]

The right balance comes, I believe, when both approaches are used simultaneously; when in the moment of, say, sitting down

---

[21] Robert Llewellyn, *Prayer and Contemplation*, Fairacres Publications 46 (SLG Press, 3rd rev. edn 2000), 53.

to pray, we drop everything in our head while consciously relaxing from the feet upwards. If we then say with our whole being, 'Into thy hands, O Lord, I commend my spirit', whatever happens after that belongs, however unlikely it may seem, to our deepening relationship with God, to the secret converse of our soul with our Maker.

And it is secret converse—secret even from ourselves. Precisely because God is silence, as John the Solitary says, it is not possible for us, who know only how to interpret sounds, to have much more idea of what is going on behind our screen of monkey-chatter, which continues at the ordinary level of consciousness, than anyone else; nor can we understand why, if the chatter should be blessedly suspended, the light doze we may fall into is more refreshing than several hours' sleep—though it has truly been, in Father Gilbert Shaw's lovely phrase, 'a resting in the love of God'.[22] But while our mind remains restless in a multiplicity of thoughts, it is desirable to keep presenting it with a single counter-thought. I quote again from the paper by Kallistos Ware:

> It is surely evident to each one of us that we cannot halt the inward flow of images and thoughts by a crude exertion of will-power. It is of little or no value to say to ourselves, 'Stop thinking'; we might as well say, 'Stop breathing'. 'The rational mind cannot rest idle', insists St Mark the Monk. How then are we to achieve spiritual poverty and inner silence? Although we cannot make the never-idle intelligence desist altogether from its restlessness, what we can do is to simplify and unify its activity by continually repeating a short formula of prayer. The flow of images and thoughts will persist, but we shall be enabled gradually to detach ourselves from it. The repeated invocation will help us to 'let go' the thought presented to us by our conscious or subconscious self. This 'letting

---

[22] Father Gilbert Shaw was Warden of the Sisters of the Love of God from 1963 until his death in 1967.

go' seems to correspond to what Evagrius had in view when he spoke of prayer as a 'laying aside of thoughts'—not a savage conflict, not a ruthless campaign of furious aggression, but a gentle yet persistent act of detachment.[23]

'By their fruits shall ye know them.' Indeed, but let us think not of our fruits (we cannot be sure about *our* fruits until we are safely dead!) but of the fruits of those who have gone before, and I find myself returning again to that anonymous saying: 'If you spend half an hour gently returning your mind to God, you will have spent the time very well.'

---

[23] Ware, 'Silence in Prayer', 35.

Silence in Action

If we want to understand silence in prayer we must look to the kingdom within, to the indwelling Christ. If we want to understand silence in action we must look at the Lord of the Gospels, at the Incarnate Christ who 'secretly, in the midst of the silence … leapt down from his royal throne' (Wis. 18:15), and from that amazing moment continued to speak his all-powerful words from the midst of the silence until the final return and the last words, spoken from the all-embracing silence of the cross: 'Into your hands I commend my spirit' (Luke 23:46).

In Jesus we see a perfect balance between inner silence and outer activity; in him we see silence in activity and activity in silence. It is to this balance and this permeation of one into the other that we aspire and to the gaining of which our lives should be directed. Apart from our times of silent prayer, the Divine Office also halts our activity and returns us at regular intervals to the wellsprings of silence. This alternation between activity and the silence of the Psalter enables us to become 'anchored to eternal silence as a ship is anchored to the sea-bed'.[24] As Max Picard put it, 'whenever a man begins to speak, the word comes from silence at each new beginning.'[25] He goes on to say:

> The man whose nature is … possessed by silence moves out
> from the silence into the outside world. The silence is central

24 Maharishi Mahesh Yogi, *On the Bhagavad-Gita* (Penguin Books, 1969), 226, 369.
25 Max Picard, *The World of Silence* (Henry Regnery Company, 1964), 8.

in the man. In the world of silence movement is not directly
from one man to another but from the silence in one man to
the silence in the other … A man in whom the substance of silence is … an active force carries the silence into every
movement. His movements, therefore, do not jolt violently
against each other; they are borne by the silence; they are
simply the waves of silence.[26]

'The silence is central in the man.' The Gospels speak of
the silence of Jesus in every incident. They convey vividly the
impression that, whenever he begins to speak, the word 'comes
from silence at each new beginning'. We can *hear* the silence before he says, 'Simon, I have something to say to you' (Luke
7:40); we can both hear and see his silent gaze at a man before
he says, 'Follow me', or 'your faith has made you well' (Matt.
9:22, Mark 10:52, Luke 8:48 and 17:19). The *active* power of
Jesus's silence is astonishing. But there is another side to it, the
passive power, which is even more astonishing. Consider his silence when the woman

> who was a sinner … stood behind him at his feet, weeping,
> and began to bathe his feet with her tears and to dry them with
> her hair. Then she continued kissing his feet and anointing
> them with the ointment. (Luke 7:37–8).

The attention in this story naturally focusses on the woman and
what she is *doing so* that we are liable to miss the significance of
Jesus's part and what he is *being*. But imagine yourself in Jesus's
place for a moment: a disreputable woman, kissing your feet,
and at a respectable dinner-party too! The very thought is
enough to make anyone blush deep purple and to set up an
inner chatter so deafening that nothing else would stand much
chance of being heard.

---

[26] Max Picard, *The World of Silence*, 49, 51; this and the above quoted in
Paul Maréchal, 'Transcendental Meditation and its Potential Value in
the Monastic Life', *Cistercian Studies Quarterly* 8/3 (1973), 210–37.

'Why are you frightened, and why do doubts arise in your hearts?' (Luke 24:38), Jesus asked his disciples when he appeared to them after his resurrection. A question of immense significance, I think, for it indicates the measure of inner silence and tranquillity he requires of them in the face of the unexpected, even in the face of an apparition, as they then thought. His expectations would hardly be less in a situation like the one with the weeping woman.

A priest celebrating the Eucharist is, it seems to me, the perfect 'icon' of silence in action. So, also, the picture of the Lord having his feet washed with tears provides another icon for silence in action. But in the first we see the active side of silence in action, and in all such works as celebrating, preaching, and evangelization of any kind, the role of the priest to mediate the active Christ is easily understood. In the second we are given a model for the mediation of the passive Christ—and this is much less easily understood. How should we understand it?

In the story of the woman at Jesus's feet we are clearly presented with a further stage of his ministry to her. He has, we may assume, already *acted* in relation to her, either by casting out the seven devils of Luke chapter 8, or by liberating her with the command, 'Go your way, and from now on do not sin again' (John 8:11), or in some other way. Whatever it was, it was only one half of the complete cure. His ministry to her must continue if what has been begun in her is not to be spoiled and stunted; what is now required of him is that he be *passive* in relation to her, that he receive in simplicity and stillness the consequences of the effect he has had on her. And, of course, being who he is, he is able to. May we be spared from ever having so much required!

In less dramatic forms, the priest is constantly being required to be passive as a consequence of having been effectively active. The priest may, for instance, preach a sermon which pierces the heart of a member of their congregation. But then they may fail in the moment of being thanked for it. We do, alas, find it difficult to be praised, especially if our own parents and teachers have taken the line that praise only leads to swelled heads so that we grow up quite unfitted to receive it naturally: souls are at stake and God is at work, and self-consciousness is inappropriate.

However, it is not only self-consciousness that prevents the exercise of the passive side of ministry. There is always the fear, when faced with a reaction which threatens to overstep conventionally-accepted limits, 'Where is this going to lead?' I once heard a wise man asked the question: 'How does one avoid getting involved with people?' and the answer came back immediately: 'Give them your full attention.' I repeated this later to a priest. After a moment's thought he agreed and, by way of illustration, told me that some time earlier one of his parishioners had taken it into her head to fall in love with him. 'Me!' he exclaimed, pointing at himself with a modesty which, it must be admitted, was not entirely unjustified. But, being a man of sense, he took her out to lunch and told her that this must stop. An hour or so of his full attention effected a complete cure.

A quite different story but an example of the healing power of full attention, this time accompanied by silence as well, was that of a hospital matron to whom it fell to break the news to a young man, newly-married, that his wife had just died. She did not tell him but simply took him to her office and sat with him, neither speaking a word. After twenty minutes or so he rose to his feet. 'Thank you', he said, 'I have never felt so consoled in my life.'

That matron was an exceptional person, but I am sure one of the reasons for the power of some medical professionals, and for the queues of patients both in hospitals and the waiting-rooms of any GP, is that by and large those who work in medicine, despite the overburdened system within which they work, are not afraid to give their full attention, however briefly, to their patients. The tendency among those who undertake the priestly role but fail in this respect is noted by Jesus in the Parable of the Good Samaritan. If we take it that a *soul* is being talked about and not a body, the story becomes not only comprehensible but of daily occurrence. The priest and the Levite looked but they did not *see* a soul stripped and wounded and half dead. Perhaps what they did see was an aggressive man, irritatingly over-opinionated; or an attractive woman, too sophisticated to embarrass a poor clergyman with the wounds life had inflicted on her. In any case, whatever kind of person they saw it was not a kind which, to their unpenetrating gaze, stood in need of help. Thank heaven for the many signs that these things are being better understood and that the clergy are immeasurably more open to all sorts and conditions of people than they were even ten years ago.

In Matthew 5 there is a little collection of four very hard sayings indeed (vv. 38–42), all of which are answers to the question, 'How does one avoid getting involved with people?'. The one which says, in effect, 'give them your full attention' is: '… if anyone forces you to go one mile, go also the second mile' (Matt. 5:41). But all four are directives concerning the passive aspect of ministry:

> Do not resist an evildoer. But if anyone strikes you on the right cheek, turn the other also; and if anyone wants to sue you and take your coat, give your cloak as well … Give to everyone who begs from you, and do not refuse anyone who wants to borrow from you. (Matt. 5:39–40 and 42)

Hard sayings; but what is hard about them is the *thought* of them. The actual practice turns out to be not only surprisingly easy but has results which are precisely contrary to those we expect, sending our smiter or borrower happily on their way, released from their needs in relation to us. Such experiences delight and refresh the soul and yet remain elusive because knowledge—even knowledge gained from experience—is never enough. What is always necessary is to remain 'anchored to eternal silence as a ship is anchored to the sea-bed'. For the essence of full attention is inner silence. Without inner silence the passive side of ministry cannot be developed; and if it is not developed we will always be too busy, too entangled in situations, to develop ourselves and so be able to help others in their development.

Jean Vanier founded the L'Arche communities for mentally handicapped people, and from a chapter in his book *Community and Growth* called 'Welcome' come the following three passages which are closely connected with silence in action:

> Sometimes when people knock at my door I ask them in and we talk, but I make it clear to them in a thousand small ways that I am busy, that I have other things to do. The door of my office is open, but the door of my heart is closed. I still have a lot to learn and a long way to go. When we welcome people, we open the door of our heart to them and give them space within it. And if we have other things to do which really can't wait, we should say so—but open our heart all the same.[27]

> It is always a risk to welcome anyone. It is always disturbing. But did not Jesus come precisely to disturb our routines, comforts and apathy? We need constant stimulation if we are not to become dependent on security and comfort, if we are to continue to progress from the slavery of sin and egoism towards the promised land of liberation. To welcome is not primarily to open the doors of our house. It is to open the doors of our hearts and become vulnerable. It is a spirit, an inner attitude. It means accepting the other into ourselves,

---

[27] Jean Vanier, *Community and Growth* (Paulist Press, 1979), 195.

even if this means insecurity. It is to be concerned for others, attentive towards them, and to help them find their place in the Community or in life itself. To welcome means even more than to listen.[28]

The first welcome is very often the important one. People can flee because it has put them off. Others stay because of a smile or an initial act of kindness. People should not be made to feel that they are upsetting things when they arrive. They should be able to feel that we are happy to share with them. We have to know how to respond sympathetically to a letter or a phone call, how to add a personal note of gratuity. If we really welcome each new person as a gift of God, and as His messenger, we will be more loving and open.[29]

You will notice, however, that Vanier in those passages is not quite making the point I think Jesus is making in the saying, 'if anyone forces you to go one mile, go also the second mile'. Vanier is concerned with what we are doing to the other; Jesus, it seems to me, is here concerned first with what we are doing to ourselves. He wants us to be free of other people so that we can be free for God, free to pray, to intercede, to praise, to stand in silence before him, to grow in our relationship with him. In order to be free of others we must give them *more* not less than they ask for. There is a tough realism rooted in a spiritual law in these four sayings which it is hard for us to grasp because our idea of what Christianity is about tends to be shot through with sentimentality, and sentimentality is the enemy of true compassion and effective action.

The passive aspect of ministry, then, is the other, and too often neglected, side of the active aspect. Both are equally important; both depend for their value on the quality of the metal in which they are cast. The concluding paragraph of the SLG

---

[28] Vanier, *Community and Growth*, 197.
[29] Idem, 199.

Rule gives a directive which, although addressed to a monastic community, has an application for every Christian:

> While the spirit of silence serves to separate each individual life unto God[,] the spirit of love must ever be binding all together in God, that in the unity of the Spirit all may seek their perfection by holy charity.[30]

---

[30] SLG Rule, Ch. 26: 'The Spirit of Love'.

SLG PRESS PUBLICATIONS

www.slgpress.co.uk